Intentional Networking
Your Guide to Word of Mouth
Marketing Greatness

Joseph Novara

Dear Adam,

Thank You!

Joe Novara

6/21/17

JOSEPH NOVARA

DEDICATION

This book is dedicated to my precious daughters, Sophia and Isabella. I love you both with all my heart. Thank you for all your encouragement as I take this journey.

JOSEPH NOVARA

CONTENTS

PART TWO: All About Referral Partnerships

PART THREE: Three Happy Stories To Close Us Out

INTRODUCTION

I'm a connector. I always have been. I am not saying that I always did it well, but I always did it. I was an especially poor connector when it came to connecting friends with what I hoped would be romantic opportunities. One friend had his heart broken so bad; it's been 20 years and I still don't think he has forgiven me. I make a point of never setting my friends up with dates anymore. I'll save that for the match making websites.

The kind of connections I'm talking about making are business connections. Making business connections can be so easy, but so many people are apprehensive about making them. What are the issues? Fear of making a bad connection? Not sure who a good connection will be? Still embarrassed from a bad connection in the past? Or, maybe it's just plain laziness. There are so many reasons people give for not making connections. But one of the biggest excuses I hear people give for not making connections is that they just don't know the people to connect with others.

How can that be?

Oh wait. I know. You're not out meeting new people with which to make connections for others. Of course, you're not going to be able to make connections for others if you're keeping yourself isolated from other business owners and professionals. How are people going to connect you to others if they don't know you either? You've got to be visible as well. Then you ask, "What am I expected to do? I have a business to run."

Or, a sales professional might say, "I have numbers I'm expected to reach every month. How am I going to have time to meet new people when I'm out making cold calls."

That is true. You do have a business to run. You have numbers to reach. That is why I wrote this book. When you learn how to network effectively and become a connector, your reach of new businesses will increase faster and more dramatically than it would if you knocked on every businesses door within a twenty-five mile radius of your business. The same holds true if you are in Direct Sales with one of the many MLM's (multi-level marketing).

However, if you only go to networking events without a system to follow, you will certainly find yourself equally frustrated with your struggle to develop new business. I have been there. I had gone to networking event after networking event for a long time without any luck. After speaking to a mentor of mine, it became clear to me that, while networking is extremely important, I was going to have to create a system for collecting and connecting the business owners and sales professionals I was meeting.

It took me years to develop my system. A system that has proven to work when followed and implemented. I also feel very confident in the techniques I have learned and developed over the years. In the pages that follow, I am going to share these systems and techniques with you so you don't have to create your own. I have also intentionally made this an easy to read book. I have read some books on networking that were written so pretentiously and with such difficult systems to follow, you would have thought you were reading the manual for building your own Space Shuttle. No, my belief is, keep it simple. There is no reason networking and connecting have to be difficult. As a matter of fact, networking and connecting should be enjoyable.

When two people call or email you with the news that a connection you made is a great success, the joy you feel will be incredible. I know. I have been the giver of many of those connections, and it always feels good.

JOSEPH NOVARA

PART ONE

All About Networking

JOSEPH NOVARA

Chapter One

The Go To Guy

There are many different sales and marketing methods a business professional can use to bring in new business. I have been in sales for almost 25 years. I have sold graphic design services, real estate in downtown Brooklyn and a lot of printing. The majority of my sales career has been in the print industry. I have used many of the methods known for sales and marketing. Telephone cold calls. In person Cold calls. Newspaper ads. Radio Ads. University Directory ads. Telephone book ads. Signage. Posters. Sponsoring events. Social media. Website, and on and on. I spent more money on marketing than I would have ever believed possible.

A website and a solid social media plan are necessities in the market today. Many of those other marketing techniques are not quite as necessary. Well, except cold calling, but there's not much fun in that, unless you're a glutton for punishment. I have done my share it, but I certainly don't love it.

I have found Networking to be the most effective sales strategy for my business. However, it wasn't always that way. Before I learned how to network effectively, I struggled like many people do. I would go to networking events and leave without any new business. I collected plenty of business cards, but I didn't know how to network effectively. Luckily, I had developed follow up skills from my years of selling real estate and cold calling. Once I began to apply the follow-up skills I had learned to the contacts I was developing while networking, I saw a drastic increase in new clients.

I had to develop systems of follow-up and most important; I had to stick to those systems. I also had to become known as "The Go To Guy." Do you need a painter? I know just the guy. Do you need a new CPA. I know just the woman. Do you need a new home built? I know the perfect company for you. I am the guy you call when you need something. I know who to call. The good thing about being "The Go To Guy" is when someone needs my service; I'm the first person that comes to their mind.

I developed effective systems for making connections. Referrals are a great way to let people know you appreciate them. The law of reciprocity means that eventually that appreciation will come back to me. I get many referrals from people that just want to say thank you for the many referrals I have passed to them. People want to get referrals for me. Quite often I've been a good source of business for them, so it only makes sense.

The majority of my new business comes from networking and has for many years. I can't imagine my sales and marketing plan without having networking as one of its primary action items. Maybe **THE** Primary action item.

Chapter Two

Dancing Fool

By nature, I'm generally a shy and introverted person. Sure, I'll be the guy to crack the jokes at the party. But it better be a party where I know a lot of people. Otherwise, this guy goes from being the jokester to the quiet observer. Then those awkward feelings of not knowing where to stand or sit begin to plague me. "Maybe if I just keep sipping this glass of water, nobody will notice that I'm not saying a word." However, put me in a business networking event, and I know why I'm there. I'm on a mission. I'm there to make new business connections. I'm there to develop new referral partnerships. I'm also there to help my current referral partners connect with new people.

Just be yourself. Be authentic and behave with the greatest integrity. If that's not good enough for people you meet, then move on. There will surely be someone at the event that will.

About 20 years ago, I was invited to a New Year's Eve dance and dinner party. I honestly believed I would be able to overcome the shy guy and get out on the dance floor to dance. What I envisioned and what actually happened were two entirely different events. When I first arrived, I was completely overwhelmed by how many people were there. Some I knew; most I did not know. I immediately felt overcome with insecurity.

The dinner was upstairs, and the dancing was on the floor directly below. After eating dinner and talking to a few people I knew, I decided it was time for me to go down to the dance floor. I put it off for as long as I could, but I couldn't put it off any longer. As I walked down the stairs, I could hear the music pumping. Through the doorway at the bottom of the stairs, I could see the room was dark with the pulsing of a strobe light.

You would have thought I was walking down into a pit of hungry lions with the anxiety I felt. When I first got downstairs, I immediately found the first dark corner where I could hide. I eventually came out a little, but I mostly stood with my back against the wall. I had become a wallflower. I was kind of moving to the beat. Moving my knees up and down, but not committing to dancing. God forbid anybody should see me.

I was very disappointed that I had succumbed to the fear. I really wanted to dance, but fear was preventing me from doing it. Then a life-changing event occurred. My friend Clarissa came over to me and asked me why I wasn't dancing. In most circumstances I would not have been honest with her, but for some reason, I was with her. I told her I felt stupid dancing. Clarissa said, "Joe, everybody here is more concerned with how they look than how you look." I want to repeat that for you. "Everybody here is more concerned with how they look than how you look." That was mind blowing for me. That statement changed the way I look at groups ever since. I'm not saying I don't feel anxiety when I go into a big networking event. Every once in a while, I just want to turn around and walk right back out. But I don't. I stay and I network. Like Clarissa said, everybody there is more concerned with how they look than how I look.

Notes

_____

_____

_____

_____

_____

_____

_____

_____

_____

_____

_____

_____

_____

_____

_____

_____

_____

_____

Chapter Three

The Networking Jitters

I met with my friend Heather recently for coffee. I was hoping to learn a little more about her and what she is doing to grow her business. She owns a specialty contracting business that focuses on making renovations in the homes of disabled people. Heather is so passionate about helping people. Her business is still in its first year, so relying on prior business as her sole referral source is out of the question. I have always been impressed by how outgoing Heather is. She's funny. She's witty and unafraid to throw a jab back when a jab has been thrown at her. I like Heather very much. I admire Heather.

Another thing about Heather is that she literally gets sick when going into large networking meetings. Her stomach gets nauseous and the idea of speaking to people she doesn't know scares the daylights out of her. Seriously! This is the woman I admire and am so impressed by. I was surprised to hear this.

Here's the funny thing. When I told Heather that I often feel very uncomfortable at networking meetings and would rather sit in a corner with my cup of coffee, she was as surprised to hear me say that as I was about her.

Networking can be very intimidating, even for the most seasoned networker. But like Heather and me, you must not let that stop you. Many people that go to networking events are frightened. People are afraid of looking like a fool. Of embarrassing themselves. They're afraid others won't take them seriously or will look down their noses at the services being offered. People are afraid of rejection or, even worse, of being ignored.

These are just feelings, and feelings aren't facts. Again, they are just feelings.

I am not saying we shouldn't honor who we are, but what I am saying is that we should never, ever allow fear to dictate what we do and where we go. When Michael Jordan was cut from his high school basketball team, he didn't go home and quit forever. Instead, he looked fear in the eye and said NO WAY! The following season, instead of saying, "I'm too embarrassed to go to tryouts", or "Everyone will laugh at me for getting cut from the team last year," Michael Jordan said, "Bring it On!!!!" We all know how that story turned out and continues to go.

Do you believe that you don't have the same spark within you as Michael Jordan does? If you don't believe you do, then you are dead wrong. We all have that spark inside of us. We all have a fire inside of us waiting to blaze.

So now you might be saying, "Sure, sure. That's fine for you, Mr. Motivation, but it doesn't work that way for me!" Again, I say you are just being hard on yourself. I was so quiet as a teenager, a girl I knew from my neighborhood used to call me retarded and would make fun of me incessantly for being so quiet. At dances I was a consummate wallflower, only wishing and praying I could go out and dance. I stopped playing sports in school because I became afraid of what all the other kids thought of me. As I became a young adult, crowds were a recipe for panic attacks and anxiety. This went on for many years.

Then the day came when I said NO MORE! I am not going to allow fear to rule my life anymore. No, no, no! I took baby steps. I learned how to grow my comfort zone instead of watch it shrink.

Do you want to grow your comfort zone? It's easy. Do one thing you're afraid of doing a couple of times a month. I'm not saying you should go jumping out of airplanes, unless that's your thing. But I am saying, do something that makes you a little uncomfortable. Something you feel some fear and maybe embarrassment around. Expand your comfort zone.

When I bought my first business, I began attending networking events. I began to put myself into situations that normally would cause me anxiety. These situations still caused me anxiety, but I moved through it. I developed a strategy. Breathe, meet someone new. Breathe, talk. Breathe, move around the room looking for someone else to speak to. Breathe, join a conversation already in process.

Over time, this became a little easier and even enjoyable. I began to see business increasing. People began to know my name around the business community. I also developed a reputation as a connector. I made such a point of developing relationships through networking; I was quite often the go to guy when you needed a name. I still am.

So like my friend Heather, don't let fear stop you from going out and making those new connections you need for growing your business. Each time you face that fear of social situations, it lessens and your word of mouth business continues to grow.

Chapter Four
Set Some Goals and Enjoy Yourself

I'd be lying to you if I told you I didn't feel some anxiety when I walk into a networking event, but I'm there on a mission. I ascertain my goals long before I get to a networking event. The last thing I want to do is walk into a room full of people I don't know and then start trying to formulate a plan. I can assure you; at that point it is not going to happen.

Like me, some of you are more introverted. Not the outgoing types. You know you need to go to networking events to build your business, but you're not comfortable talking to people you don't know. First of all, don't worry. There are probably more people like you at the event than you realize. Some have mastered their fear and have learned how to strike up conversations with people they don't know, others have not. If you're one of the people that have not gotten this figured out yet, then I'm talking to you. If you've got it all figured out, please read along and pray for those of us that still struggle.

23

Once you start going to more and more networking events, you will begin to see many familiar faces, but in the beginning, you may know very few, if any people at all. That can be a bit stressful for even the most seasoned networker. Call or email the organizer of the event to find out if you can bring a guest with you. If you can, that's great. Ask a friend, a colleague, your spouse, ask anybody. Bring a wingman. Just don't bring someone who is painfully shy. That would defeat the purpose.

When you attend networking events, it is very important that you avoid "The Friend Trap." As you go to more networking events, you'll begin to see many of the same people. Some of those people will begin to be your clients or referral partners. Some will even become your friends. You'll walk into an event and have people saying hello to you first. That feels good. But don't be that person that goes to the networking events and only talks to people you know because it just feels more comfortable. Remember, there was a time when you walked into a networking event, and you didn't know anybody.

If it's a networking group I regularly attend, my goal is to meet two people I've either never met before or haven't had a chance to have a proper conversation with. What's a proper conversation you ask? A proper conversation is more than just saying hello and moving on. I ask questions. I get to know the person. How long has she been in business? What got her into the business she's in? What kind of clients does she work with? Is she from around here or has she moved here from someplace else?

If it's a networking event that's for a special occasion or just one I have never been to before, my goal is to meet, at minimum five people I have never met before. And I'm not talking about the servers or the bartender working at the event. I'm talking about those business owners and decision makers that will help grow my business. In order for that new connection to count towards my goal, I either schedule a future meeting with that person or at the least I get a commitment from them that when I call, we will schedule a time to meet. I make sure I get their business card. I also make sure I give them my business card.

I make sure that while I am speaking to my friends or referral partners, when one of my new prospects walks by, I call them over and make introductions to whomever I'm with. I want this person to know I am someone who knows many people, and I will be a good resource for them down the line. I've only known this person a few minutes, and I'm already trying to help them. Do you think they remembered me the next time they needed my services? Of course they did!

Notes

_____

_____

_____

_____

_____

_____

_____

_____

_____

_____

_____

_____

_____

_____

_____

_____

_____

_____

Chapter Five

A Little Investigative Work Goes a Long Way. A Very Long Way.

Preplanning for a networking doesn't have to be difficult. First of all, make sure you have your business cards and a pen. The pen is for writing small notes on the new prospects business card to remind you of a conversation you may have had with them or to follow up on a promise you may have made. Always follow through on your promises.

Many networking events have sponsor tables. Do a little investigating ahead of time and find out who the sponsors are going to be. Then go to those companies' websites to learn more about them. It will look good for you if you can approach the sponsor already knowing some information about who they are and what they represent, making this a case where cyber stalking can pay off handsomely.

Some events are created using online companies to invite people. You might be able to check online to see who has confirmed they will be attending. Use this list to your advantage. You can start

27

working the room before you even get to the event. You can look up the Linkedin profiles of each of these individuals to know whom to target ahead of time. Also look at their contacts. If one of the people going to the event happens to be connected on Linkedin to someone you know, you may want to reach out to your contact to find out a little more about your prospect.

I have had great success with developing new business by learning about the organization hosting the event. The hosting organization has worked hard to put this event on and to acknowledge their hard work can go a long way. Read Chapter 19, titled "Finding Karen." I knew ahead of time particularly who I wanted to meet, why I wanted to meet her and the lengths I took to meet her.

A little preparation pays off. A lot of preparation almost guarantees success.

Chapter Six

This Is Not The Floor Of The New York Stock Exchange

When I am at a networking event, I am there for one reason and one reason only. I want to increase my business. Helping others increase their business is a bonus.

It would be great if I could walk around the event with a notepad and just take orders.

Some business people mistake a Networking Event with the floor of the New York Stock Exchange. Wouldn't it be nice to be at the event, going from one person to the next with your notebook taking orders?

"You'll take one in blue. Great. And you want three in yellow. Oh, and Mr. Smith, I'll have your order ready tomorrow."

It doesn't work that way.

Unfortunately many business people go to a networking event, and when they don't walk away with an order, they feel they have wasted their time and refuse to go to another networking event, regardless of who's catering it.

So how do I increase my business if I'm not getting orders? It's easy. Help others get what they want. Work hard at being interested, not interesting. There will be plenty of time for you talk about yourself. Listen to your new prospect. What is their business? How did they get into their business? Ask them, "Where are you from?" "How long have you lived here?" Find things that you have in common and share short stories to identify. Don't take over the conversation. You're building a relationship and what do all the best counselors preach on relationships. Listen, listen, listen.

When it looks like the conversation is coming to an end, politely tell your new prospect, "I'd love the opportunity to speak to you some more. Would you mind if I called you next week to get some time on the schedule?" More than likely, the prospect is going to say yes. Ask for their business card and then offer yours.

One thing to keep in mind is that your prospect may turn the tables on you and start asking all the questions. Either your prospect is uncomfortable answering questions about themselves or, you are now being prospected. If that's the case, dive right in. Be genuine, be honest and be professional. What we are trying to do here is to lead our prospect into asking us how they can help us. Of course, we need to get business.

There are many different ways that business can come to us. It may come through the prospect himself, or our prospect may know someone that needs our product or service. Whatever it may be, allow the prospect to feel like they have done you an incredible service by either giving you the business himself or by helping you to come in contact with a potential buyer. In either case, send a note card, hand written, to say Thank You. I can't express how important it is that your note arrive handwritten. It shows the buyer or referral source that you truly appreciate what they have done. An email is not nearly as good, but it beats nothing at all. Always say, "Thank You" - preferably with a handwritten card or note.

Notes

_____

_____

_____

_____

_____

_____

_____

_____

_____

_____

_____

_____

_____

_____

_____

_____

_____

Chapter Seven

How Do I Turn A Networking Event Into More Business?

A lot of people say they are going to networking events to try to get business, but they only end up talking to their friends for the two to three hours they are at the event. That's fine if you have all the business you need. I've never been that lucky. I always go to a networking event with a pocket full of business cards. I don't walk around handing out my card to every person I meet, but the night may come when every person I meet is solid gold, and I don't want to be short on business cards should that night come.

I described my goal setting technique for networking events in Chapter four, titled, "Set Some Goals and Enjoy Yourself". If it's an event I regularly attend, my goal is to meet two people I've never met before, or at the least have never had a proper conversation with. If it's a networking event I've never been to before, my goal is to meet at least five people I've never met before. I turn off the shy guy inside me and let my true self come out. I smile. I say hello and offer to shake hands with whomever it is I am meeting. I want to know as much about them as I can

33

know in a five to ten-minute conversation. I'll get my opportunity to tell them all about me. We're going to meet at some point. Whether it's for coffee or a visit at his office. Then I can tell him more about who I am. How I got into my business. Why I love doing what I'm doing. There will be plenty of time for that. But right now, I want to know about him.

When he and I meet in a week or two, I may know some of his interests and can cut out an article I see that makes me think of him. I want to show him I was listening attentively when we first met. That goes a very long way. I am so appreciative when somebody listens to me and remembers obscure things I may have said. It makes me feel important. Well, guess what, I'm not the only person that feels that way. Many people feel that way. Listen to what people are saying to you. It will be appreciated.

When you have coffee, you need to set up some kind of a plan. How can you help him get business? What kind of business is he looking for? Who are good people you can introduce him to? You may already have an idea of people you can introduce him to ahead of time. That's great. Call these contacts ahead of time and ask them for permission to make this introduction. Your referral partners will always be ready for your call that you're going to be making an introduction to them with a new prospect. Your new prospect doesn't know this yet, but he is going to find out soon.

When your prospect asks you how he can help you, be prepared. Don't say, "Well, I didn't think about that." That would be JUST PLAIN CRAZY! You're not Mother Theresa. This meeting is about relationship building. A relationship that will eventually help you to make more money. And there's nothing wrong with making more money. So, after he asks you how he can help you, tell him. Have at least three different types of industries you know his business is involved in at the tip of your tongue. Tell him you would like to meet decision makers in these industries. Then you go for the big hit. You ask him if he can introduce you to the decision maker in his company. You may have to prove yourself a little before he makes that introduction. After he has had positive encounters with the introductions you've made for him, he'll be more than happy to introduce you to the decision makers at his company.

Notes

Chapter Eight

Elevator Speech Olympics

You don't have to beat your prospects over the head with a club and drag them away

When that opportunity does arise for you to share what you do with a prospect, I can't express this enough. Keep it short and sweet. You want to have your elevator pitch prepared and ready to give that one-two punch. Your elevator pitch should leave your prospect confident about what it is you do and wanting to know more about who you are and how you do it. An elevator pitch should only be about 20 to 30 seconds long.

Have you ever heard one of those elevator pitches that leave you completely unsure of what the other person actually does or if they even have a job at all?

Here's an example.......

Bob is at a networking event, and he is trying to build his contact base. Over by the dessert table, Bob sees a woman standing by herself looking a little lonely. Bob uses this as an opportunity to meet someone new. He introduces himself. The woman introduces herself as Carmen. After some small talk, Bob asks Carmen a question.

Bob: So Carmen, what do you do for a living?

Carmen: I help people realize their dreams.

Bob is now intrigued.

Bob: Oh yeah, how do you do that?

Carmen: Most people live their lives thinking they know what they want, and are always disappointed when they finally acquire what they believed were their dreams only to find out they were wrong. My proven technique first helps people realize what their actual dream is and then I help them go for it.

Bob is a little confused now. He's not sure yet what the proven technique is, but he's sure Carmen will tell him in a moment.

Carmen: As people age, they look to their retirement and wonder if they will be able to survive. Have they invested enough? Will they leave a lasting legacy for their children?

Bob is very confused now and wishes he had never stopped to speak to Carmen.

Carmen: My second step is helping them overcome the fear of failure so they can crash through the barriers that are preventing them from experiencing their truest dreams. You see, whether it's owning real estate or becoming a graphic designer or seeing their grandchildren more often, I want to open their minds to possibilities……

And Carmen goes on and on into oblivion. Bob never does actually find out what Carmen does. Nor does Carmen ever find out what Bob does either.

Has this ever happened to you? Is this you? If it is, develop an elevator pitch that is clear and gets to the point. Please, JUST GET TO THE POINT!!!!!!

Sales Coach Brian Keith McNeill of Greensboro, NC has a very effective method for developing a clear, understandable elevator pitch in three easy steps. Here is exactly how Brian teaches it in his seminars and training.

01. You know how...... *(Introduce a problem you can solve.)*

02. Well, what I do is...... *(Introduce yourself as a solution.)*

03. So that they can...... *(Payoff that they are looking for.)*

Example number 1:

You know how some people are unsure how to or are fearful about purchasing a home for themselves?

Well, what I do is gently walk them through the home buying process by asking them questions and being receptive to their

39

answers......

So that they can live in the home of their dreams and feel good about how they got there.

Example number 2:

You know how every business you meet is fighting for the number one position on Google?

Well, what I do is through analytics and research, I find out what are the best methods of search engine optimization being used within my client's industry. I then develop and implement an SEO strategy on my client's website....

So that my client gets greater exposure on the internet, which will then drive more business their way.

Chapter Nine
Please Watch What You Say!!!

When we attend Networking Events, A sure fire way to turn off a potential new client is to start talking about politics. Sure, you may know everyone's name in the House of Representatives. Maybe you can even list off every bill they've ever voted on, but the minute you start expressing opinions, you may as well put your coat on, go home and kiss that prospect you were talking to goodbye. You may get lucky and find out that you and the prospect share the same views, but is that a risk you're willing to take? Not me. I stay as far away from politics as I can.

As a matter of fact, there are people who will try to rope you in. They do a little fishing. They might drop a negative comment here, and a sarcastic comment there related to politics. Don't take the bait. If you feel like you're in a position where you have to give an answer, say "Hmmm, that's a very interesting point. I usually try to not let politics bother me one way, or another, so I don't have much of an opinion one way or the other." Then try to change the subject.

But please, please make sure you don't change the subject to sex. Yes, there are a lot of funny things you can say and share about sex, but many people find any talk about sex offensive, even when it's meant to be light and funny. Memorize a few clean jokes. Everybody likes to laugh. Even the biggest sourpuss enjoys a good laugh. If that sour puss is your prospect, and you make them laugh, BINGO! You may have hit a home run right then and there. But do not talk about sex and do not talk about politics. While we're at it, let's stay away from talking about religion as well.

Chapter Ten
Last Call.....For Alcohol

I remember one particular high profile business networking event. It was being held in an Italian Restaurant. The food was phenomenal – the meatballs were especially tasty. I had a plate of baked ziti that was to die for, and the Italian bread was soft and warm, which melted the butter I spread on it.

There was a woman in attendance; we'll call her Lisa. She was (and still is) a pretty important representative for a bank. I have known Lisa for several years, and I like her. However, I could never in good conscience give Lisa my business. Each time I see Lisa at business events, she starts out very charming. She always dresses very nicely – she looks like a million bucks. Unfortunately, if alcohol is being served, by half way through the event, Lisa is slurring her words. That was the case (again) that night at the Italian restaurant. Lisa begins acting silly and at times says things that are inappropriate or mean. I'm not saying she's drunk; I'm just saying she's a different person after she just had a few drinks.

Business events can be very stressful. Especially if you don't like crowds. You should Have Fun Networking, however if you're not capable of stopping after one or two drinks, then wait until after the event to have a drink. If you normally get tipsy after one or two drinks, then skip the beer or wine they're serving at the function and have a soda or water instead. You're not there hanging out with your friends. You're there to get business. Not lose it.

In his book, "The Little Black Book of Connections," Jeffrey Gitomer suggests that you give out your competitor's business card if you plan on getting tipsy at a networking event. Instead, I suggest you wait until the event is over, and you're home safe before opening that bottle.

Chapter Eleven

Eating Like a King, Or Not Eating At All. It's Up To You

Networking meetings that feature food are my favorite. Most of the time, its really good food. Local restaurants get to show what they're known for, which is an added plus.

However, not all networking events provide free food. Sometimes, there is a charge for the food or there may be no food available at all. Don't be afraid to contact the person in charge of the event, just to make sure. If you can't find the contact information for the event organizer and you're concerned you may be hungry, then I suggest you have a light snack beforehand.

Here's a scenario you don't want to experience.

I had been invited to a networking event that was being hailed as the event to beat all events.

The two gentlemen putting on the event sent out multiple emails with the heading "You Don't Want To Miss This One!!!" They also advertised on the websites of two different chambers of commerce.

I couldn't wait! I was very excited to see what they had in store for us. Great food? A wonderful environment? Giveaways? The suspense was killing me!

Finally, it was the night of the event, and I arrived about thirty minutes late. It was being held in one of the conference rooms of a local hotel. I found the room where the event was being held and entered. The room was anything but festive. In fact, the room was dimly lit; almost depressing. It was a very large room, and there were not many people there, so it made the room look even emptier. I walked around and spoke to a few people. Everyone appeared to be as disappointed as I was. But wait! It gets better!

We could have excused the dimly lit room. We could have dismissed the lack of festivities. But what was inexcusable was the poor food selection: raw broccoli crowns, carrot sticks and crackers. Oh, and don't let me forget the cheese spread! Drinks consisted of a couple of cases of bottled water and several bottles of wine, which were to be served in Dixie cups. Dixie cups!

I found out that most people who arrived earlier had already left. It was easy to see why. Honestly, I found it quite amusing and an incredible lesson to be learned. Ok, so none of the advertisements or emails ever mentioned anything about food. They did mention wine.

However, based on the title "You Don't Want To Miss This One!!!," we all just assumed there would be really good food.

Wrong!

Had I emailed or called one of the two guys putting this event together to ask what kind of food was being served, I would have known to have a snack before arriving. I was hungry when I arrived and was expecting dinner - not raw broccoli and carrots! I left shortly after I arrived and treated myself to a cheeseburger. Lesson learned. Never assume!

Notes

Chapter Twelve

Join In On The Conversation

Many times when we are at networking events, there will be two people talking. Of course, one of those people is somebody we've been dying to talk to. What to do? Do I behave rudely and interrupt their conversation? Do I follow my prospect around the event like a stalker until I see my opportunity to strike? Or do I just say forget it and walk away? Sadly, most people just walk away.

Why are you at this event? You're there to Network.

Why is the person you hope to speak to also at this event? This person is there to network as well.

So what I would tell you is just go and network.

You don't have to be rude. Walk right up and stand there for a moment. If you see an opportunity to join in the conversation, do so. Don't take the conversation over and show everybody how smart you are. Just be a part of it. Most likely, after a minute or two, there will be an opportunity for you to introduce yourself.

Make sure you introduce yourself to everyone in the conversation. If you only introduce yourself to the person you are trying to meet, you will not only look rude to your prospect, you will also have offended a possible future business contact. The others in the conversation may also prove to be useful to you at a future time.

During the course of the conversation, and at an appropriate time, ask each person for a business card. Make certain you are prepared to hand each of them a business card of your own. As they give you their card, you hand them yours and say thank you each time. If at all possible pay your prospects business card praises. Our business card is an important part of our identity. Getting a compliment on our business card can go a long way. When someone says, "Wow, you have a really nice business card!" It's like they're telling me, "Wow, you sure are handsome!" I know I have a nice business card, but I sure do like to hear it too.

Nothing irritates me more than to have someone interrupt my conversation with someone else and then pretend that I'm not even there. First of all, it doesn't get any ruder than that. Second, I will never, ever give that person a referral or any of my own business. Sometimes, the only way to deal with someone like that is just to walk away. Unless it's a very important conversation, you can pick up with the person you were speaking with later. There's no reason to get into an argument. You're there to network and enjoy yourself. We are going to run into jerks at different places and times of our lives. I find it always feels better to just move on and not let their poor behavior have an effect on me.

So remember, when attending an event that has a networking element to it, focus more on listening. I like to follow the Who, What, Where, When, Why and How model (WWWWWH). When you are trying to learn about a new prospect, you can keep him talking all night if you keep asking questions that start with one of the WWWWWH's. Start off with these six questions:

"Who do you work for?"

"What do you do there?"

"Where is the business located?"

"When did you start at this company?"

"Why do you do work in this profession?"

"How long have you been doing it?"

Now you have the first six questions to start a conversation with almost anyone you meet when networking. If you find yourself stuck during a conversation, try to think of a question that could start with one of the WWWWWH's.

Notes

Chapter Thirteen

What If I Get Snubbed?

Sometimes adult life is going to be just like high school. There are the cool kids. There are the dorks. There are the kids with money. There are the kids with no money. There are the kids that fit in with everybody, and then there are those kids that don't seem to fit in with anybody. That's just life. When we go to networking events, you could walk around the room and pick out each of those groups, except in more grown up bodies. Be a much more mature version of yourself despite how other people may act.

When you are at networking events, every once in a while you come across the "no-networking" zone. That's the spot where two or more people are congregating at a networking event, but don't want anyone else to join in on their conversation. You walk over, and they ignore you. As a matter of fact, they may even turn a little bit away from you. Let's acknowledge first and foremost, yes, your feelings have been hurt, and you may like to leave right now. Don't. There could be a number of reasons you've been "snubbed." Number one is that they may have been waiting a long time for this opportunity to speak to each other and don't want any interruptions. If that is the case, they should take the conversation to a more quiet location and avoid giving others the wrong idea, but they haven't, so just move on.

Another reason could be that they don't even realize you're there. Or, they just may be inconsiderate snobs and would you really want to do business with them? Do not let a situation like that ruin your time. There are plenty of other people there to talk to. Go talk to one of them.

If you're feeling embarrassed after the snub, go talk to someone you already know for a couple of minutes, just till you feel a little better. Then go find someone new you haven't spoken to before and continue building your contact list.

Let's talk a little about body language here. When you approached the two people that ignored you, it is very possible that their body language was that of not wanting to be disturbed. When two people are facing each other directly so that their shoulders are square to each other, that is a posture of not wanting to be disturbed. If it is three or more people speaking and they are standing in a closed circle, that is also a posture of not wanting to be disturbed.

If two people are standing in a V formation while speaking, that usually means they are open to others joining the conversation. When you approach, it doesn't mean they will immediately stop and acknowledge you. Be patient. They will either acknowledge you when the opportunity arises, or they or you will simply find an opportunity to join in on the conversation.

This same idea holds true if three or more people are speaking, and are open to others joining in the conversation. The group will form either a very loose circle with openings for you to step into or they may even be standing in a U formation. Again, be patient. You'll get in on the conversation.

Notes

Chapter Fourteen

Humans To The Left.
Monkeys To The Right

I've met people at networking events that once they begin speaking; I can't believe they have ever made a single dollar. I'm not referring to levels of education because I am far from a highly educated guy. However, using slang or foul language can be one of the biggest turnoffs when you're trying to get business from someone you've never before met. I'm not saying you should not be yourself. If you're not your authentic self, that will come out at some point. What I am saying is if you want to be treated professionally, act professionally.

In 1985, everybody was quite surprised by the level of intelligence Dee Snider of the heavy metal band Twisted Sister displayed when he addressed The U.S. Senate during the PMRC hearings. Everyone expected some foul-mouthed Neanderthal. Instead they were presented with a well-spoken passionate individual that made his case very clearly. Based on his highly professional speech, Dee Snider was taken very seriously.

Also, we all like to look smart. When possible, try to avoid using too much industry jargon. I had a boss once who used to tell me, "Joe, know your audience." If you start using words that your prospect doesn't understand, you could potentially create a distance between yourself and your prospect.

Chapter Fifteen

Photo I.D. Not Required. But A Business Card Is

Not having a business card or some other piece of material that will allow others to contact you not only looks unprofessional, but it gives others the impression that you're less interested in learning about the person you're speaking to and most interested in selling your own products or services. People will tire of that real fast. We are all human and will make mistakes. Even during my days as the owner of a printing business, I had even forgotten business cards once. There were always those couple of wise guys that took great joy in pointing out that the printer had left his business cards back in the office.

If you promise to follow up and get someone your information, do it as soon as you get back to your office. You want everyone to know you as someone that does what he says he is going to do. If you can't follow up on something as simple as that, can you be trusted to follow up on future business. If you're reading this, my guess is yes, you can. Otherwise, you wouldn't be a person that invests in themselves.

Notes

Chapter Sixteen
The Batters Circle

A few years ago, I had been invited to a Durham Bulls baseball game. The Bulls were down three to one. They had men on first and third, and it was the bottom of the eighth. There was a batter at the plate. A couple of minutes earlier, I noticed when he should have been warming up off to the side; he took a couple of swings with his bat, but really wasn't exerting himself at all. As a matter of fact, his swings looked pretty lazy. I'm guessing the only reason he was doing those warm up swings at all was because it was expected.

When the batter got to the plate, the pitcher threw two balls. Then a strike. The batter foul tipped the next pitch. The pitcher threw another ball. We now had three balls, two strikes. The next pitch was thrown right down the middle. It was a home run pitch. The batter swung and connected with the ball. It was up. It was up and approached the left field wall. Then the ball began to fall out of the sky, right into the left fielder's mitt.

While the first batter was at the plate, I noticed the next batter was warming up off to the side. He had a big red donut on his bat. He swung practice swings multiple times. I lost count only because I was also watching the batter at the plate. He warmed up almost the entire time the batter was at the plate. When it was his turn to get up to the plate, he approached the plate and did what appeared to be his ritual. He rubbed a little dirt on the hands. He banged his bat on each cleat. Rubbed his hands again. Then he took his stance. The first pitch came. He didn't swing. Strike one. He knew that wasn't his pitch. The next two pitches, he didn't swing. A ball and another strike. The fourth pitch was going to be his pitch. The pitcher wound up and threw a beautiful curve ball. The batter swung and connected. The crack of the ball hitting the bat was such a lovely sound. The ball blasted through the air and sailed over the left field wall, out of the park. Homerun! The Bulls won the game four to three.

There are many times when I walk into a networking event; I just don't feel like I want to start mingling immediately. I'm cold and not ready to network. I need some warming up. If there are sponsors at the event, that is a great opportunity to warm up. Sponsors pay to have a spot at these events and want to talk to as many people as they can so as to feel like they have gotten their money's worth. Go talk to a couple of the sponsors. Break up that internal ice you may be feeling. A little conversation with someone who really wants to talk to you can go a long way in helping you to relax and get on your game. You see, just like that batter warming up, you may need some warming up before approaching that big prospect. You want to be focused and ready when you swing for that home run. Get loose and connect with all the power you have.

Chapter Seventeen

The Absentminded Networker

If you are going out to represent your company or a line of products you are selling, know what you are talking about or don't bother walking out the front door. I can't stress how important it is that you know those services or products inside and out. You don't have to have a price list memorized, but know so much about the products that the person asking perceives you as an expert.

I met a woman at a networking event one time who did exactly the opposite. First, let me start off by saying she was beautiful. She was dressed extremely well, was tall and appeared very confident. She was representing a line of health and beauty products, which she claimed were the best on the market. Considering the hundreds, if not thousands of other health product lines on the market, I felt that was a pretty bold statement. However, if they are the best on the market and she could tell me why, I might be convinced to switch from the company where I was currently getting my vitamins and other health products. (If you've seen any pictures of me, you can tell I am not buying any beauty products).

I asked her what made the products she was selling better than the ones I was currently getting. She told me that these products have been scientifically tested and were engineered for maximum performance and health. Okay, that sounded like an elevator pitch to me. However, it did not answer my question. I asked, "Have these products gotten FDA approval"? She said she didn't know. I asked my first question again, except in a different way. Using her words, I asked, "How are your products being engineered differently to provide greater performance and health"? Again, she said she didn't know and that I would have to ask the scientists working on the products.

I realized I was meeting a dead end. During the remainder of the conversation, I came to find out she had been a model, but left the business and was pursuing a career in sales. I have to say, although she seemed like a pleasant enough person, I would have great difficulty purchasing any of the products she was selling based on her lack of knowledge about the products.

On the other hand, here is a completely different scenario:

I know two female business owners in North Carolina who sell health products for competing companies. Each of these ladies knows the products they are selling in such great detail, you would think they developed the products themselves. Each can quote verbatim, all the scientific testing done and the proven health benefits of these products as well as outside studies to prove the effectiveness of the products. I have been completely convinced by both, so I buy a little from each of these ladies.

Know what you are selling like you know the back of your hand.

If you happen to be presented with a question you can't immediately answer, let the person asking know you are going to find out and then do so quickly. Then contact that person with the answer. It helps build your credibility. There should be very little about the business you are representing that you don't know. We live in the information age and knowledge is always at the tip of our fingers.

Notes

Chapter Eighteen
Move Along. Nothing To See Here

It's so wonderful when we get that opportunity to speak to that decision maker we've been hoping to speak to for so long. However, you don't want to spend your whole night speaking to only one person.

Or, how about that guy that won't stop talking? He keeps going on and on while never giving you a chance to get in a word.

There are different ways to address these situations. The person you've been waiting a long time to talk to is probably much like you are and will want to meet other people as well. After a five to ten-minute conversation, tell him how nice it was to talk to him. You've already given him your business card and either set an appointment or have gotten permission to call, so just let him know that you look forward to speaking with him again soon. Shake hands and move on. However, if the opportunity arises to introduce him to one of your referral partners at the event, don't hesitate to do so. Better yet, should the opportunity arise for you to make an introduction to a new business prospect for him, do so. You will be a hero.

The guy who won't stop talking is a different issue altogether. I understand he may just be nervous and so happy to have someone else to engage with, the thought of letting you walk away seems frightening beyond words. Of course, you can't let that stop you from networking. You have a great opportunity to introduce your new friend to other people. Find out who a good connection is for this scared fellow, and help him make some connections. Give him some networking pointers.

If it's only your second or third networking meeting, the chances are good that you may have one or two more events under your belt than your new friend. You can teach him what you learned at your last meeting. You're helping him to be a step ahead.

Most times, unfortunately, The Unstoppable Talker just wants to hear himself talk and talk and talk. He could care less what you have to say, where you work, that you were just given a week to live or anything else for that matter. He has a lot to say, and he is going to say it.

There are a number of different things you can try using to break free from the Unstoppable Talker. The first is, regardless of whether he's done speaking or not, when there is a period at the end of a sentence, quickly say, "It's been nice talking to you. Do you mind if I give you a call? Maybe we could grab a coffee and talk some more." I know, it's very unlikely you will call, but it's also important you break free. Most times they will just walk away in search of a new victim.

Of course, you can always say, with a sense of urgency, "I have to go to the restroom. Excuse me." I suggest, for the sake of integrity, you head to the restroom at that point.

Sometimes, I just say to the other person, "You're not going to get any new business standing here talking to me all night. Why don't we catch up later?" I have yet to have someone tell me I am wrong after I made that statement.

Here is a sad fact; The Unstoppable Talker will most likely forget ever having met you when you see him at another networking event. If you let him get your ear, he will probably tell you everything verbatim that he told you the last time he cornered you, so I suggest you avoid him like the plague.

Whether you network for business or enjoy going out with friends to parties or bars, you will eventually come across an Unstoppable Talker. Use these tried and true techniques for breaking free. I stand by them.

Notes

_____

_____

_____

_____

_____

_____

_____

_____

_____

_____

_____

_____

_____

_____

_____

_____

_____

Chapter Nineteen

Finding Karen

Networking does something that thousands of dollars of marketing may never do. It puts you face to face with other business owners and decision makers.

I had been trying to land a big account for months when I owned my printing company. The account is a beauty school with locations all over the world. The marketing department for the organization was located within the school closest to my company. Through a little bit of investigation, I found out the name of the marketing director, Karen Bailey. The funny thing was that nobody in my networking circles seemed to know much about her, only her name.

She didn't have a Linkedin page and at the time of writing this, she still doesn't. I was going to have to do some good old-fashioned cold calling. It was a beautiful day out, the perfect day to land a new client. Arriving at the beauty school, I was equipped with a pad with my company's logo and contact info as a gift. I had my notepad and business card in hand. I opened the door and entered. I approached the customer service counter. There was a young woman standing behind the counter donned with black hair, black t-shirt & black jeans. She had several piercings on her face. My wife had been a punk rocker growing up so I knew we would be able to find common ground quickly.

"Hi, sorry to bother you, My name is Joe. I own a printing company in the area, and I was wondering if I can speak to Karen?" I asked very nicely.

The young woman answered "NO! KAREN IS NOT HERE NOW!"

Did I say she answered me? I meant to say she yelled at me. I was in shock.

I asked carefully, "Do you expect her back today?"

"I DON'T KNOW!" She barked.

I was hesitant to leave a notepad. She didn't deserve my notepad, but I left it regardless with a business card. I asked her to please give the card and notepad to Karen.

I wasn't sure how to approach this situation again. I waited a few weeks in the hopes that when I went back, the angry young punk would have since been fired. The big day was here. I psyched myself up to walk in and own the place. I walked in and there she was, the angry punkette in black, just waiting to tear my head off again. I wanted to sneak back out, but she saw me and I had to approach. I hoped she would be nicer this time.

"Hi, I don't know if you remember me, but I'm Joe. I own a printing company in the neighborhood. Is Karen available?"

"KAREN'S IN A MEETING!" She barked again. Other people were looking, and I felt embarrassed. I handed her another business card and left.

I was determined not to let this young, angry woman beat me. I would meet Karen if it were the last thing I did. Over the next several months, I stopped in once a month. Every time I stopped in, she yelled at me. She was never even the slightest bit pleasant. Every time was a different excuse."

"KAREN'S IN A MEETING! KAREN'S AT LUNCH! KAREN'S HOME SICK! KAREN'S CLIMBING THE HIMALAYAS!"

Month after month the abuse continued and month after month, I stopped in to get just a little more.

Then, a very magical day arrived. I had been invited to a networking event that was to be held at none other than this beauty school. They wanted to showcase the school and the students. I knew this was going to be a wonderful opportunity.

My goal that night was to meet Karen. Nothing else. Meet Karen.

The staff and the students were all wearing black t-shirts with white nametags. I walked around looking for Karen. I read every nametag I saw. She's not Karen, she's not Karen, he's not Karen, and she's not Karen. I even asked some of the staff if Karen was there. All but one said they didn't know. A male student indicated he had seen her earlier but that she may have left already. "I don't think this is her thing." He said.

After a little more searching, I began to give up hope. It was pointless, and I was wasting my time. I decided to change my focus for the night and meet a couple of new people. Towards the end of the evening, the CFO of the beauty school's organization gave a short presentation. He shared their mission, values and vision of the school. He shared what the future held for the school and what great things we could expect.

The thought crossed my mind that I should go speak to him. As soon as he was done speaking to us I went over and introduced myself.

"Hi Patrick. I'm Joe. Thank you for hosting this event tonight. Your team is doing a great job."

He said thank you and then asked me about my company. I told him a little bit about my business, but I also knew time was short and that someone would soon call him away.

I said, "I know tonight is not the night, but is there a time when I might be able to call you to discuss how we might be able to do some business together?"

Without any hesitancy, Patrick put up a hand and said, "I'm not the person you'd want to speak to about doing business with us. Come with me."

Patrick walked me across the room to where very few people were congregating. We approached a blonde haired woman wearing a red sweater and sitting alone. He introduced us. "Joe, I would like you to meet Karen." I smiled.

"Karen, this is Joe. He owns a local printing company and was hoping to talk to you about his services."

I thanked Patrick for helping me, and I thanked him again for the wonderful event. Then he was off to say goodnight to the other guests as they were leaving.

I could see the embarrassment in Karen's face. I decided to not use this as an opportunity to tell her about the torture I had been put through trying to meet her. I didn't tell her I wanted the 7000 business cards back that I had dropped off over the past several months. No, I acted like today was the first time I had ever heard of Karen and that I was just happy to meet her. Karen and I set up a time to meet within a week.

When I went to meet officially with Karen, the angry girl behind the counter didn't yell at me. She didn't talk to me either. When I told her I had an appointment with Karen, she called Karen to tell her "The printer is here." She then spoke to the next client as if I was invisible. Although she didn't yell at the client, she wasn't very friendly either, and that was okay by me. I was here to see Karen. Mission accomplished. Within a week of meeting Karen, I had my first order. Within six months, I was doing business with the schools across the entire country.

Being persistent was incredibly important. Not letting the angry girl get the best of me was equally as important and even helped to thicken my skin, a lot.

The best part of this entire story is that I had been personally delivered to Karen by the CFO himself. It doesn't get any better than that. That was a high-level introduction only because I took a little time out of my day to go to a networking event. Like I said, networking puts you face to face with the business owners and decision makers that will help grow your business.

Notes

_____

_____

_____

_____

_____

_____

_____

_____

_____

_____

_____

_____

_____

_____

_____

_____

_____

Chapter Twenty
Track Your Progress Like A Champ

There may be a particular networking event that you attend every month, quarter or year. Your time is extremely valuable so if you're not experiencing success from a particular event over the course of time, you may want to consider focusing your energy on a different activity when that event comes around, like cleaning off the desk in your office or doing your laundry.

Measuring the success from a particular networking event can appear very difficult. However it is not – if you use a contact management system. This is a system to capture and organize contact information, and then track all of your activities related to that contact. You must input every touch you make to the contact into your system. I start tracking my contacts right after I leave a networking event.

As you do more networking and consistently grow your contact list, you will accumulate a lot of business cards. If you're not careful, you will end up with stacks of business cards, which will eventually end up with rubber bands around them and tossed into a drawer.

Here's how you handle this fortunate situation right away before it becomes an unfortunate situation.

Put the business cards into three categories. A, B & C prospects.

A Prospects are people you are very likely to business with right away, or they may be doing business with one of your competitors and just need some persuading on your part.
• Send a hand written Thank You Card within 24 hours of the event. Be sure you don't include your business card with the note. You gave them a business card already when you first met them, and you don't want this note to feel like a marketing piece.
Instead, this note card is personal. In the note card, write a very simple message like, "It was very nice to meet you at *insert event*. I would really like to buy you a cup of coffee. I will reach out to you in the next day or two.

As you promised in the note card, call within a day or two. Quite often, people are so impressed that you have sent a hand written note card, they might call you first. Don't wait for your prospect to call however. Schedule a meeting as soon as possible.

Follow up is key here. After your meeting or follow-up meetings, call once every month to check in. Most sales transactions don't happen until around the fifth touch.

After you've been given permission, send your online newsletter if you have one (If you don't, consider starting one). Introduce your new prospects to other professionals in your network. Learn their birthdays, the name of their spouse and children, their likes and their dislikes.

B Prospects are people that may do business with you or at least could be valuable connections for your referral partners. Do the following with B Prospects.

• Send a nice to meet you email within 24 hours of the event. The email should say something like, "It was nice to meet you at *insert event*. I would like to get together for a cup of coffee." Also mention a couple of times and locations that are convenient for you. Again, after you've been given permission, send your online newsletter. Call once every three to four months to check in. Drop by their place of business if you're in the neighborhood. It's okay to have coffee with the contact, but don't make it a habit. Save that time for your A Prospects.

C Prospects are people that you will unlikely ever get or give business to; however, you don't want to ignore them.

• Send a nice to meet you email within 24 hours of the event. The email should read something like, "It was nice to meet you at *insert event*. I hope to see you again soon." With permission, send them your online newsletter if applicable. If there is business activity with the C Prospect, move them up to a B or an A. Otherwise, send them emails once or twice a year just to stay connected. If a C Prospect invites you to coffee, seriously consider asking them what the agenda would be. If it sounds like they are just trying to fill time in their day, thank them for the invitation and politely decline. You might them know you will be very busy for the next couple of months.

Now comes the fun part. Inputting the names into my Contact Management System (also called CRM's). I want to input the prospects name, business name, phone number, business address, email address, and where or how I met this wonderful prospect into my CRM. I have alerts set up to remind me when I am suppose to call a particular prospect or stop by a prospects place of business or simply send my prospect an email. The money is in the follow-up!

There are many different CRM's you can purchase. Some are extremely detailed and may work for your business, but my suggestion is always to follow the KISS system. Not the four guys wearing crazy makeup. The KISS system of Keep It Simple Silly. My system works very well for me, but it may not work for you. Find something that works for you and use it. That's the most important part of the system. Using it.

Make sure that whatever system you work with has places for you to input referrals and orders received. This helps indicate if I am experiencing success. I don't want to beat a dead horse. If this person is not a good referral source, I need to focus my energies on more fruitful contacts. I don't completely eliminate that person from my list. They may awaken from the dead some day and surprise me with a return phone call. It's happened many times.

On the contrary, you also want to track who your superstars are and keep them very happy.

Chapter Twenty One

A Cold Night Of Networking Warms Up

I was at a business networking event recently. I have to admit; I didn't feel like a star networker that night! First of all, I don't drink alcohol, and this event was in a liquor distillery. The selection of alcoholic beverages far outnumbered the non-alcoholic options.

As a matter of fact, after standing in a ten-minute-long drink line, I was finally up to the bar. I asked for a coke. The bartender said they didn't have any sodas. I could see about twenty bottles of sparkling water behind the bar. I told the bartender, "I'll just have a sparkling water."

His response was, "The sparkling water is for mixed drinks only."

I may have been a little rough in how I expressed my unhappiness about this to the bartender. He did give me the cup of sparkling water, but I can assure you I didn't make a friend.

To shake it off, I went out to do some networking. For some reason, I just couldn't seem to get in the groove. I felt like each person I was talking to was either there for social reasons or would not be someone my business could connect with. I pressed on however. There was a business owner I am acquainted with, named Tim. He was speaking to two people I didn't know. Their body language was open for other people to join in the conversation, so I approached. Tim immediately introduced me and I joined in the conversation. One of the people was a doctor with her own practice. That was very encouraging. I thought, "She is someone I can certainly help with getting new clients and as a physician, I'm sure her office does some printing." Our conversation went well. Other people eventually joined in the conversations, and I realized at some point that it was time for me to move on.

I met a few other people and learned about their businesses, but I honestly just didn't feel like I was connecting with anyone. I was talking, but I didn't feel any connection. During one particular conversation I was having with a small group of people, a fellow business owner I know joined in on our conversation. Without any prompting, he began expressing to everyone in the small group that he finds my services on the internet for a quarter of what I charge. He wasn't doing it to be mean. He is "just like that." He turned off each of the people in that group of five, who proceeded to walk away with a bad taste in their mouth and a bit of embarrassment for me. I would be lying if I said I wasn't a angry; I let it go and finished off the evening speaking to a friend of mine for the final thirty minutes of the event.

When I left, I asked myself if I had gotten any real value out of the event. I honestly felt like I had not. The food had been good, and I got to see a couple of friends, so I decided to leave it at that.

Following my normal system, the next day I sent emails to the people I had met at the networking event. I said it had been nice to meet them. If there was something I could point out from our conversation, I made sure to bring it up in the email, although briefly. I didn't ask for anything. I only said, "I hope to see you again soon."

That night, I was working in my home office. It was after six and dinner was almost ready. Friday night is pizza night in the Novara house, and it was Friday. I was looking forward to some pizza.

My cell phone rang. It was a number I didn't recognize, but I decided to answer it. It happened to be one of the people I had met at the networking event the night before. We had spoken for five minutes at the most, but he seemed like a very nice man.

"Hi Joe. This is Charlie. We met last night at the chamber event. I sell real estate, if you remember."

"Hi Charlie. Of course, I remember you. I sent you an email earlier today. I hope you received it," I responded.

"I did receive it. Joe, my wife, owns a business that is moving locations next week. One of the things they have forgotten to take care of is getting their stationary and marketing material printed with the new address. I got a good feeling from you last night. When I received your email today, I knew you would be the right guy to help my wife out of this mess. I'm going to put her on the phone now."

Charlie put his wife on the phone, and we scheduled a time to meet. Within a few days, she put in a very large printing order.

Did I get more value from that event than just a free meal and some good conversation? Absolutely! Most times, things aren't as bad as they first appear.

The moral of this story was in the follow-up. Follow-up is the number key to success when growing a business by word of mouth.

Chapter Twenty Two
Fishing For Whales And Snapper

You have the ability to turn one lead into business at almost every networking event you go to. That doesn't mean you're going to have closed business immediately after you call a lead. Some leads take weeks, months, maybe even years to pay off sometimes. Yes, that's right. Years. If the payoff is big enough, years may be worth waiting. Look at some of the biggest business deals in modern history. Many of the giant mergers we read about in the news take years to close, but the results often show great pay days for shareholders and everyone closely involved. Do you think they minded waiting years? Be patient for those bigger payoffs. They will come. They will happen if you're patient.

The smaller business happens faster. You get a fast return, but it's also considerably smaller. That's why it's good to have a mix of business coming in. I wish I could say I treated my smaller clients as well as I did my larger clients, but that has not always been the case. If I had to take my focus away from one of the two projects, I would focus more on my larger client. The payoff is bigger and most often, longer lasting.

85

In the printing industry, I was usually lucky enough to have a team backing me up to take up any slack there may have been. However, if you're a solo-preneur, you've got to decide if you want to focus your energy and time on a lot of small deals or a couple of big deals. Of course, we all need to eat, so you have to have some of the smaller deals in the mix, but make those smaller deals the exception to the norm. We want to focus on the bigger orders.

We often work just as hard on smaller deals as we do on the larger deals. Quite often, a smaller company has more emotion involved in the business they are giving you. You may be working directly with the owner of the company. He sees this order as money that is not going into his personal income. Maybe another bill he just can't afford right now, but has to do. The larger the business you're working with, the less personal it becomes.

However, the larger the organization is, the larger the egos will be. There are politics involved, and your company could be just the political football this organization needs to punt around till one side says uncle. One side usually gives up, and the deal gets done. Probably not the way it started either, but it gets done. You waited. You were patient, and you walked away with a big pay off.

That deal may have started from stopping to say hello to someone standing by herself at the local Christmas networking event. After talking to her for a little while and helping her to feel a little more comfortable, she asks you to give her a call after the New Year. There might be an opportunity for your company with her organization. You promptly call her on January 3rd. You don't get paid on your first deal for eight months, but by the time you get paid, you have three other deals in the pipeline with her company. During those eight months, you had to let a handful of smaller deals go so you could focus on this larger company. You didn't let all the smaller deals slip through your fingers. You took care of your current clients. You had to be a little pickier about new business. The more work these smaller deals would require, you had to let them go. It wasn't easy to do, but you knew, if you could focus on this larger company while pleasing your current customer base, the payoff would be well worth it. This is not a fictitious scenario. It happens every day. Turn one lead at every networking event into closed business, but try to focus on the ones that will take longer to pay off. The wait will be well worth it.

Notes

PART TWO

All About Referral Partnerships

JOSEPH NOVARA

Chapter Twenty Three

Developing Referral Partnerships For Success

Developing referral partnerships can be fun and rewarding for all parties involved. What is a "referral partnership" you ask? To describe what a referral partnership is, I first want to tell you about one of my favorite historical stories.

The Battle of Thermopylae. The year was 480 BC. An army of 150,000 Persian soldiers was advancing to attack and annihilate Greece. King Leonidas of Greece put together an army made up of three smaller armies. Each army brought their own talents, abilities and their own special skills. When combined, this small force was a mighty machine. Approximately 7000 Greek soldiers took on 150,000 Persian Soldiers. When the Persian army advanced on Greece, King Leonidas and his small army held off the Persian soldiers for seven days, and the Greek army eventually went on to defeat the Persians. It was King Leonidas' plan to combine these three small forces into one force that made them such a force to be reckoned with.

This is very similar to how referral partnerships work. Referral partnerships are made up of non-competitive professionals going after the same client base. Each referral partner brings his own talents, her own abilities and their own special skills. They pass business back and forth between each other, even calling on clients together at times to help strengthen the proposal and overpower the competition. Referral partners also try to find their fellow partners new business before even being asked.

One summer afternoon, I had been invited to a networking event that was being held on a black top parking lot. Did I mention it was mid-July and around 95 degrees out? Well, it was.

During the event I met a woman named Kelli. Along with her husband, she had just recently opened a medical practice that specializes in the removal of spider veins and varicose veins. She and I had a great conversation. I knew that her business would be a great source of work for my business, but before I was going to ask her for some business, I wanted to help her to generate some new clients and referral sources. I thought, "Who could be a good referral source for her company"?

After asking Kelli a number of questions, it occurred to me that elderly people quite often have health issues with spider veins and varicose veins. I knew I was on to something there.

I asked her, "Are people in the senior community good referrals' for you"?

Kelli answered, "Yes. Seniors make up the majority of our client base."

Now I had something to work with. I thought of my friend Pat who is the marketing director at a senior living community. It is Pat's job to find and interview new people for the senior living community, so she meets almost everyone that lives there.

But wait a minute! The patients at Kelli's practice could also be potential candidates for Pat's senior community. I located Pat at the event and introduced her and Kelli to each other. I then explained why I was making this introduction. They were both very appreciative for the connection.

Now that I knew which kind of referrals were best for Kelli, I began to introduce her to the many people I knew in the Elder Care industry. It was very easy. I made most of the referrals via email. After writing the first email, the rest of the emails were pretty much CUT and PASTE.

The best part of this story is that I ended up getting some nice business from Kelli and her husband. The good will I have developed throughout the Elder Care community of business owners and sales professionals has been a great source of referrals and new business for all of my business ventures.

There are three basic ways I like to give a referral. The first is a step above a lead, but it is still a bonafide referral. A business person you know has made it known they are looking to meet a particular person in a company that you happen to know. You give the business person the phone number and email of the person they want to be connected to. You let this business person know they should use your name when contacting their potential prospect. I call this a cold referral.

The second type of referral, which is probably the most common, is when email connections are made introducing the two parties to each other. When making a referral this way, be sure to tell each person a little bit about the other person in the email. Let's say for instance I knew a scientist that was looking for a photographer to capture her work in photo's, my email introduction may go something like this.......

Dear Lillian,

I know you're looking for a photographer to document that great research you're working on. I want to introduce you to my friend Justin. He's a wonderful photographer, and I know the two of you will get along.

Hi Justin,

Please take good care of Lillian. This research is very important, and the fate of mankind is in Lillian's hands. I hope this is a good introduction for you both.

Take care.

Joe.

The referral is for Justin, so I expect him to follow up. Lillian may have already gotten the names of two or three other photographers,' however my recommendation of Justin will hold some weight. If he contacts Lillian right away, he stands a very good chance of getting that business.

It's also my responsibility to follow up with Lillian to confirm everything went well.

The third and best way to give a referral is to bring the two people together. You can do this in a number of ways. You can meet for lunch or coffee. You can meet at the prospective customers office. You can have them both meet at your office. Try not to meet at the office of the person you're referring the potential client to. The potential client may feel uncomfortable and defensive he's going to get teamed up on, even if that's not the intention. Try to keep the first meeting on neutral ground, if at all possible.

As the person receiving the referral, it is very important that I follow up, immediately. I don't want to embarrass my referral partner, and I certainly don't want to lose out on potential business. Sometimes, the follow up can be something as simple as an email just letting the prospective client know you will be contacting her shortly. Feel free to cc or blind cc the referral source as well in the early stages of the transaction.

It is also extremely important that as the person giving the referral, I check in on both parties from time to time during their transaction. Listening to the elation from both parties is wonderful. Their elation will certainly mean more business for you down the road. That's what referral partnerships are about.

Notes

Chapter Twenty Four

Developing Referral Partnerships: The Sequel

I love helping other people make money. I'm serious. I get a real rush out of it. The way I do it is by introducing my referral partners and my new prospects to businesses they are currently not generating business from whom they would benefit greatly from knowing.

One of my referral partners happens to be a personal injury attorney. If I want to hold up my end of the bargain, I need to get him some referrals. If I wanted, I guess I could sit in the hospital emergency room and talk to every person that looks like they could have a potential lawsuit, but that would probably be taking it too far. However, I do happen to know that chiropractors are a great source of business for personal injury attorneys. And guess what? Personal injury attorneys are great referral sources for chiropractors too. Anytime I meet a chiropractor, I think of my referral partner, the personal injury attorney. Anytime I meet a new personal injury attorney, I immediately think of the chiropractor in my referral network.

This works with many different kinds of businesses. Real estate agents make me think of my referral partner who sells and installs security systems. Estate planning attorneys make me think of my referral partner, the CPA. Property managers make me think of my referral partner in landscaping. When I meet graphic designers, I immediately think of the printers in my network. The connections are limitless.

Of course, I have expectations as well. Some of my referral partners may not be able to introduce new business to me directly, but by giving me access to their network, my window of business opportunities opens wide.

A referral partnership usually doesn't develop based on one meeting. Like most relationships, it has to grow with time.

Many of us have heard the statement, people do business with people they know, like and trust. After much thought, I realized, I don't even have to like you. However, if I'm going to do business with you, I must know and trust you. If I don't know and trust you, all bets are off. I expect you to hold me to the same standards. A referral partnership does not necessarily involve a referral fee. A referral partnership is about relationship building. Not just money. The money will come as a result of the relationship.

When I receive a referral, it is extremely important that I immediately follow up.

I take giving referrals very seriously. If one of my referral partners isn't following up with the people I'm referring him to, then I have to stop referring him business.

A situation like that happened with a referral partner who would have received guaranteed business. I have a friend named Mike that owns two restaurants. One afternoon while I was eating at one of his restaurants, Mike complained to me about his insurance carrier and the different ways they were ripping him off. I told him I had a referral partner named Robert that handles insurance and that I would have him call right away.

I called Robert. "Hey Robert, I've got guaranteed business for you. Call this number, and I think my friend will sign up today." A few days later, I called Mike, the restaurateur, and I asked him how it went. He said he hadn't heard from Robert. I thought, "That's strange." I apologized and told him I'd follow up with Robert immediately. I called Robert to ask why he hadn't called. He said he'd gotten very busy, but would call that day. Okay, great. I understand. We all get busy.

A few days later I talked to Mike. He still hadn't heard from Robert. Now I was embarrassed. I called Robert again. He said it was on his to do list. That was months ago, and to this day Robert has never called. He would have gotten immediate business for two restaurants, not to mention the network of restaurant owners Mike knows. Do you think I'm going to give Robert a referral ever again? I can assure you I won't.

During my printing career, one of my favorite referral partners was a graphic designer named Scott Bradford. I had referred countless clients to Scott, and I got thanked all the time for the work Scott did. Any print projects Scott worked on other than the ones I referred to him; he referred the print work to me. He let me know the budget I'd be working within, and he made sure I would be handling the printing. He and I each have our individual strengths. Combined, we became a much stronger force.

Chapter Twenty Five
When I Get A Referral

Poet John Lydgate wrote these words that President Abraham Lincoln later repeated: "You can please some of the people all of the time, you can please all of the people some of the time, but you can't please all of the people all of the time".

When you are given a referral, like any other order you may produce at your business, these words will ring just as true. There are going to be customers that you will just be unable to please. No amount of back bending will be good enough for them. You can give these customers everything they ask for and more, but guess what--they will still be unhappy. It happens. That's just life. What matters is how we react to these customers.

The worst occasion is when these customers come from a referral. You really want your referral source to get good reports about the experience. Here are a few things to think about before addressing this situation. First, there may come a point when you are going to have to let go of the customer. These "Negative Normans" are never going to change, or least not during the time of this particular order. If they are uselessly sucking up a lot of your time and energy, let them go before they suck more out of you. I know it's difficult to fire a customer after you've already invested so much time into them, but believe me, you will be doing yourself and the client a favor.

When I owned my printing company, I had a client for which we printed star and moon charts. She had a business that dealt in witchcraft and she had sheets printed for her customers. We printed thousands of these sheets. The problem was that every single order, without fail, was a problem. Either the colors were too dark, too light, too bright, too dull, not dark enough, not light enough, not bright enough, etc. She was emotionally draining to my entire staff. When she walked into our office, all the joy was immediately sucked out of the workplace. We reprinted a few orders for her over time thinking we would make her happy, but she always found something wrong with the reprint as well.

I began to think that we might be better off without her. It took a couple of years and many printing orders to make the decision to let her go. Then after the decision was made, it took a while to actually fire her. Fear of financial insecurity can make us behave in irrational ways sometimes, but the day did come. We printed an order for her and she complained to my staff once again that it wasn't perfect. My staff was not surprised, but they were still deflated, nonetheless. I spoke to her about the order and was able to convince her that it was in fact a well printed job.

The next time she came in to place an order, I had all her printing files, plates, and film prepared in a package for her. I explained that over the years we had never been able to please her and that I had come to the realization that it was time for her to move on to another printer. The look in her face was that of utter disbelief. The look on my staff's faces was that of relief and joy. I can't say I celebrated the separation. It actually made me nervous to let a client go, but at the same time, knowing that she wouldn't be back gave me a sense of relief as well. My point in telling this story is that there are some people we are just never going to be able to please.

It is most difficult when that person who is incapable of being satisfied comes from a referral. The way to handle this is as easy as it is difficult. No matter what you do, do not delay in calling your referral source. Your referral source needs to be made aware of the situation, in a very kind way. The conversation could go something like this, "Sammy, have you spoken to Ken about the project you referred him to us about?" Sammy will probably say no, but regardless of his answer, you should follow up with something similar to this, "First, let me say that I appreciate your referral, so this is no reflection on you, but we seem to be having a disconnect with Ken. I'm not sure why, but we are not meeting his needs and I can assure you, he is not happy with us. I'm just giving you the heads up that I'm going to suggest to Ken that he move on. I will make a couple of suggestions for companies he may call on, but Sammy, I can assure you, we are not the company for him. I'm sorry if this makes you look bad, but we have tried very hard to make this work, but it just isn't."

A few things may happen here. The first thing is the worst of the possible results. Sammy may get angry with you and express his unhappiness. If that is the case, accept that it is very unlikely that you will ever receive a referral from Sammy again. So be it. Move on to bigger and better things. The second result may be Sammy asking you if he could talk to Ken to try to work this out. He may feel that there might be something he can do to smooth this over. If Sammy asks for this opportunity, give him a shot. But give him one shot and one shot only. If Ken starts behaving the same way, break out the big scissors and cut Ken off.

Then, the third scenario could go like this, Sammy may express to you that he was afraid that this may happen. He hoped it wouldn't, but he knows Ken can be a pain in the booty sometimes. He will apologize to you and let you know that he's not angry with you and agrees that you need to do what you need to do. The third scenario is most likely the one that will occur. If Ken is a jerk, most people in his life probably know it, Sammy included. He wasn't saving it up just for you and your company. The Kens of this world behave this way everywhere they go, so it's usually not a surprise to their friends and family when other people complain about them. Regardless of how Sammy responds, send him a card to thank him again for the referral and apologize that things didn't work out.

Most referrals will not go poorly. It is up to us to deliver and deliver big. We want our referral partners to look like heroes. I have to admit, when I give a referral, I feel quite elated when I hear how well it went. The person I referred is happy and my referral partner has made some money. Win/win! We should check in at least once after we have made the referral to make sure things are going well. Post it in your calendar to give both parties a call to see how things are going. This is an opportunity for you to ask your referral partner if they have any leads for you at that time. Don't be afraid to ask. That's what developing referral partnerships are about.

I had a referral partner who is a graphic designer. I would refer business to her on a regular basis. I was in no way embarrassed to ask her for referrals. She did very well with the business I was sending to her and I needed to make sure she reciprocated. I don't say this to be unkind, but there were many other graphic designers looking for the kind of business I was referring. If my referral partner couldn't refer business back to me, I would have to move on to one that could.

That exact thing did happen with another graphic designer I had been working with. She did great work, but I struggled to get her to reciprocate. Then the day came where one of my best clients called me to complain that she was too busy to do their graphic design work at that time. Because of my introduction, they had given her a lot of business. I called the designer and she expressed the same thing to me, that she was too busy. I'm glad she was so busy. However, if she was so busy, where were the return referrals? It was time to make a change.

Luckily, I had someone to refer my client to immediately. I had seen his work already and I knew he was very talented. He had already passed me a couple of referrals, so I was happy to be able to reciprocate. He hit a home run and made me look like a champ. My clients were very happy with him and haven't looked back since.

JOSEPH NOVARA

Notes

106

JOSEPH NOVARA

Notes

Chapter Twenty Six
There Are Plenty Of Fish In The Sea

Dollars speak a lot when it comes to gauging success from a particular referral partnership. One of my former referral partners is a Business CPA, who was seeing a lot of success from the referrals I was forwarding to her. I would have thought she would in turn send referrals to me. Especially considering we were both looking for similar clients. After several months of not seeing any return, I asked her if she would introduce me to a particular client of hers. She said that it would be unethical for her to make the introduction due to client confidentiality.

I truly respect her position. However, she and I had spoken in the past regarding how she could pass referrals to me. One of my best referral partners is a corporate attorney. He often sets up a meeting between himself, myself and the referral he is connecting me to. He never makes these introductions until permission for the introduction is granted by the person he wants to introduce me to. He would set up a meeting for coffee to bring us together. After that, it is up to me to follow up with the other person.

Unfortunately, that kind of effort too much work for the CPA I had been referring business to. A few months later, another CPA I networked with introduced me to an organization that would become one of my best accounts. From that point on, I forwarded my referrals to him. He has since passed several more referrals to me that have paid off handsomely. To be quite honest with you, I never did officially break up with my other CPA referral partner. I just didn't pass referrals to her anymore. Had she asked, I would have told her why. She never asked.

Our time is valuable. We all have a limited amount of minutes on this planet. We need to make the most of those minutes. Every single one. I can't waste those minutes hoping and praying someone is going to change when they have made it fairly clear that they are not interested in changing. Most times, a dying referral partnership takes care of itself. It simply fades away.

Just don't get caught up in the trap I let myself get caught up in, which is, hoping that one day that big referral will come in from this source that has given little or nothing back to the partnership. Most partnerships do not represent a fifty-fifty give and take. Often, one person in the partnership does more of the work than the other. One person in the partnership benefits more from the relationship. That is just the way human nature works. However, don't be afraid to put an end to a referral partnership if you feel you are being taken advantage of. Like most relationships that have come to an end, there are usually plenty of other fish in the sea.

Chapter Twenty Seven
Ask And Ye Shall Receive

I remember the first time I asked one of my clients to refer me, I felt awkward and embarrassed. They are a large dental practice that does a large volume of printing. I had always provided great service, and I had a great relationship with my client. She and her entire staff liked me a lot. Why should I feel uncomfortable asking her to let other people know about my services? I did ask her, and she took it very seriously. She said she had never thought about referrals before and would give it much thought. Within a few days, through emails, she introduced me to several other dentists. Two of those referrals converted into closed business. Do you think she would have ever thought to refer me had I not taken the time to ask her? Probably not.

After that, I made a point of asking my clients to consider making referrals for me. I also promised to them that I would always do the same for their business. After all, we are talking about the law of reciprocity. These are probably the most precious referrals you can ever get. Make sure you treat this referral like gold. Not only is your client's reputation on the line, but your business relationship with this client is on the line as well.

Remember follow up, follow up, follow up. It's not difficult to follow up. If you knew that three blocks away and up the first tree on the corner was a bag of money, you would probably make sure you followed directions very carefully to find that bag of money. Treating a referral with respect and high consideration can result in you finding your bag of money. Sure, it's work. But someone referring you has taken much of the work out of the sales process already. That is worth more than months and months of newspaper advertising.

PART THREE

Three Happy Stories To Close Us Out

JOSEPH NOVARA

Chapter Twenty Eight
A Real Estate Love Story…..Not Really

When I was renting and selling real estate in Brooklyn, NY, I quickly learned the power of developing strong business relationships. When I look back now, I can not believe how important the skills of relationship development were to my career. There were so many players in the game. Let's start with the basics. First the landlords. Then there's the building superintendent, the doorman, the sellers, the management companies for co-ops and condo's, co-op and condo boards, mortgage brokers, banks, appraisers, lawyers, other real estate agents and finally, the people looking to acquire the property.

Every day was a non-stop juggling act. Some deals went smooth as silk. Some deals became such a mess, it required my relationship with every person on that list to be rock solid. You may ask, "Why would you need to involve a landlord and seller within the same deal?" I will tell you.

I was working on a deal selling a 1600 square foot two bedroom apartment with a private roof deck in a building that was being gut renovated and would be all new construction. The seller gave us an expected date for completion and closing. As a realtor, we learned to pad those numbers because the owners were always more optimistic than realistic.

My buyer was very excited and had no problem getting his $832,000 loan approved. The date for the closing was set. My buyer gave his landlord notice to move, and all was well with the world. Or so I thought. The closing date was approaching within a couple of weeks, so I stopped by the building to see how things were progressing. I was shocked to find that the construction on the apartment was only halfway completed. I called the owner to find out what was happening. He said things were going right on schedule and that we would be closing on the date we were promised.

Within a few days, the broker at the real estate agency I worked at announced to all the real estate agents and myself that we needed to alert our buyers that the closings would be delayed for at least a week. I immediately called my buyer. He was very unhappy, because this put him in a bad position having already told his landlord he would move out on a particular date. He spoke to his landlord and received approval to extend his stay for another week. I contacted his mortgage broker to let him know the closing was moved a week out from what was originally promised. He was able to get the buyer an extension. That week turned into two weeks, which turned into three weeks, which turned into four months. Not four weeks. Four months.

My buyer must have backed out of the deal twenty times over those four months. The broker at the real estate agency I represented was no help at all. We had the exclusive right to sell these apartments, so if my buyer backed out; there were several other buyers ready to jump in at the drop of a hat. The broker had nothing to lose. Only I did. I hate working very hard at something and making no money at all.

First, I was lucky enough to already have a relationship with my buyer's landlord. I called his landlord on a regular basis, keeping him informed of what was happening in the deal. Second, the new tenant the landlord had moving into the apartment was quite happy when I found him a different apartment right up the street for less rent. I also cut my broker's fee considerably to make him happy. I stayed in constant communication with my buyer, always letting him know where things stood.

Eventually, I stopped giving him closing dates because that just became ridiculous. Some days he would yell and shout. Some days he sounded like he wanted to cry and some days he sounded optimistic that the deal would go through. In the end, I had to get the seller to agree to some concessions for the buyer so he wouldn't pull out of the deal. They weren't huge concessions. He wanted an upgrade on what were already top of the line appliances and fixtures. The seller agreed after I helped him realize that my buyer had hung in there with him through the whole process. Legally the buyer could have walked away from the deal, but he didn't. We closed the deal, and he could not have been happier.

Over the next two years, the buyer sent multiple referrals my way. I was able to find a renter for his apartment within a day or two of him moving out. Also, the renter I helped relocate down the street sent me referrals during the next two years as well. It was my relationships with the seller, the buyer, the mortgage broker and the landlord that kept this deal alive. I treated every relationship during that transaction with the utmost respect and care. In the end, it paid off very well.

Chapter Twenty Nine

I Just Bought A Franchise. Now What Do I Do?

You have just purchased a franchise, and you're ready to be a business owner. You're excited and can't stop bragging to all of your friends and family what a great opportunity this is. The next several months are a little tougher than you initially anticipated. Writing big checks for attorneys, contractors, accountants, real estate broker, vendors, the franchisor and on and on. At times, it feels overwhelming. Then the training begins. The rigorous training program is filled with so much information about your new franchise business, you can't imagine stuffing one more thing into your brain, yet you manage to get in several hundred more.

Then the big day arrives. Opening day. Of course, the Franchisor has helped you prepare for marketing your opening day. It's a big day for the franchisor and fellow franchisees alike. Your first day goes exactly as planned. Of course it does. They have done these hundreds of times before. The following weeks also go as planned.

117

But then you notice something you had feared from the beginning. There isn't enough business being generated. You look over the marketing plan multiple times. You're doing everything it suggests in the book, and you just don't understand why you're falling just a little short. The franchisor makes some suggestions, most of which you have tried already. The franchisor also tells you not to worry, as this is normal. You're anxious to get this thing rolling. Sure, you can let things grow slowly, but you have a plan to open three more stores in the next five years. Waiting on business to come is not in the cards for you.

Luckily, the franchise representative that helped you with the purchase of your business had been putting you in contact with some of the other franchisees in your region. You begin calling some of them to find out their experience with growth. Most say that they had the same experience you are having, but over the course of a couple of years, things evened out, and they began making some money.

"A COUPLE OF YEARS!!!!" You yell. "I CAN'T WAIT A COUPLE OF YEARS!!!!"

But then you speak to one franchisee that says he began seeing a profit within six months. He's got your attention for sure. He explains that he learned how to develop a Word of Mouth marketing plan to grow his business. You agree to meet with him for a cup of coffee the following week to discuss this Word of Mouth marketing plan.

On the day you meet him, he's got two other fellow franchisees with him. He explains that each of them has grown their businesses at a similar pace through Word of Mouth Marketing.

Okay, the suspense is killing you, and you demand to know what in the world Word of Mouth Marketing is. Each of the three other franchise owners goes on to explain that traditional marketing clearly wasn't working. And while they were getting some benefit from their online presence, it just wasn't enough.

One of the three franchisees explained that when she was a mortgage broker, she found great benefit through networking. She did so well as a mortgage broker; she had no problem coming up with her deposit for the down payment for her business. She went on to explain that after opening the franchise and business wasn't growing as fast as she would like; she put on her networking shoes and began doing what had been so successful for her before. She began to network.

The franchisee you were originally meeting for coffee chimes in here. "I would never have learned about networking had I not made phone calls to other franchise owners just like you did. That's how the three of us met."

The three owners tag teamed in explaining how they had to learn the law of reciprocity. If they were going to grow their own business, they would have to help others grow their businesses first.

You begin to learn how to locate networking meetings to attend. You learn how to give and get referrals. It gets explained very assertively that when you receive a referral, you must treat it like gold. The person who gave you the referral has a reputation at stake as well.

They teach you how to identify good referral sources for those you come into contact with. "You want to become the Go To guy," they explain to you. "You want your name to be the first name people think of when they need anything. When they need your services, your name will be the first they think of also."

Over the next couple of weeks, they meet with you two more times and help you devise a plan. One of your new friends even goes with you to a couple of networking events to help you warm up. There's nothing wrong with bringing a wingman along you figure.

Things go better than you expected. Immediately you meet a Chiropractor. You remember how your brother in law, the Personal Injury Attorney has said many times that chiropractors are great sources of business for him. You assume it's got to work the same way for the chiropractor too. You promise to introduce him to your brother in law. They got along so well; they begin passing business back and forth between each other.

You do this with other people you're meeting as well. Over the coming weeks, as you attend more networking events and help other people get business, you begin to see many of these people showing up at your business. Then people begin showing up saying that someone you had met at a networking event suggested they come. There's a real buzz around the community about you now. Everybody's talking about you and your business.

Eventually, you join a Networking organization, like BNI, where your business is exclusive within that particular group. No one else can join the group that does what you do. Of course, you did your research and picked a BNI chapter that would be strong for your business. You also wanted to make sure you were in a chapter that you would feel comfortable passing referrals to the other professionals within the group.

Things are picking up very nicely for your business. As a matter of fact, at the end of year one, you have exceeded your financial goal. Not by a lot, but by enough that you recognize the power a Word of Mouth Marketing plan can have for a business.

Once a month, you meet with the other three franchisees to discuss new ways to improve the plan. You have each invited other franchisees to meet with your group to learn how to grow their business through Word of Mouth Marketing. Most are either skeptical or just too busy. One or two try to make a stab at networking, but they go in with a "me first" attitude. When they don't see immediate results, they quit and complain that networking is just a big waste of time. You smile and wish them well. You don't have time to sit and listen to complaints. You're off to a networking event. Some poor professional may be in need of a referral, and you're just the person to pass it.

Notes

Chapter Thirty

The CPA

I have a friend who is a CPA. For many years, she has had a successful practice and has never had to go out looking for new clientele. In November of 2011, shortly before the start of Tax Season, Caroline received a bad medical report. Actually, the news was quite devastating: breast cancer. Caroline was in complete shock. With tax season just beginning, this was not the kind of news she expected, nor wanted to hear. She was what appeared to be, very healthy.

With her husband and three teenage daughters at her side, Caroline went through Chemo, radiation and a double mastectomy. There were complications and Caroline experienced a much longer recovery than anticipated. While all this was going on, Caroline's CPA practice dwindled down to almost nothing. She was eventually able to go back to work, but she had no clients to work with.

In December of 2012, Caroline went to work for another CPA to help out for the upcoming tax season. Caroline did so well and helped the other CPA so much that when April 15th passed, he offered Caroline a full partnership. However, the understanding was that Caroline would have to bring a certain percentage of new clients over the next year and an additional number of clients over the coming years in order for the partnership to continue. Caroline saw this as a great opportunity. Either way, she was going to have to bring in new clients if she was going to start her own practice again.

Caroline was faced with a situation she had never faced before, going out and getting new clients. We met for coffee on a Monday morning, and Caroline explained to me that she was very concerned that she would not be able to get new clients. She had never had to prospect before and had absolutely no idea how or where to start. She complained that she is not a salesperson. I let her talk and cry about not being able to take on this task. She contemplated the idea of working for a franchise accounting company. I waited until I felt she was ready to listen.

"How many new clients do you need to bring before next tax season?" I asked.

Caroline answered "Thirteen."

That's thirteen new clients in eight months. I asked Caroline if that was possible. She explained that it was very possible for someone that knows sales and marketing. Again, she reminded me that she knows nothing about either.

I explained to Caroline, "We're going to do some Networking. I think you will do very well as a networker. We will help build you a network of clients and referral partners that will blow that thirteen number out of the water."

I took out a sheet of paper, and I asked Caroline to write down the names of ten of her former clients. After she had written down the names, we developed a letter to reach out to these former clients. In the letter, Caroline explained that she is back in action and in great health. She understands that they are working with new CPA's and hopes they are very happy where they are now. What she asked each former client for were referrals to other people in their spheres of influence. Caroline explained she would call on a certain date and time to discuss.

Caroline was very surprised by the response she received. Of the ten letters Caroline sent out, only two of the former clients could not be available to speak to Caroline. Seven out of the remaining eight made referrals to multiple new contacts and two of the former clients rehired Caroline as their CPA. Caroline was off to a good start. Of the multiple referrals Caroline received, over the course of the next several months, Caroline was able to convert four of those referrals into new clients.

Caroline didn't wait for the phone to ring. We still had to reach that thirteen. For a month, Caroline went to multiple networking meetings to get a feel for the professionals attending. At first she was very scared and shy. I went with her to several meetings when she first started going and introduced her to as many people as I could whom I thought could be of help building her business. Caroline found some of the meetings very helpful. Some she found were not her cup of tea.

Caroline also visited several exclusive networking organizations, such as BNI, which allow only one member per occupation. The investment to join the group of $500 was tough, considering she was still fighting her way back, but she looked at it for exactly what it was. An investment. She narrowed down her choices, joined a BNI chapter and became a very visible, active member.

Caroline also became active at the Chamber of Commerce. She volunteered at events when she could. She attended most of their networking events. Caroline was becoming very visible. People were talking about Caroline everywhere. She began to know many people in the business community and began referring people in the business community every chance she had.

Developing referral partnerships became very helpful in building Caroline's business. She developed alliances with other non-competitive professionals that were going after the same target clients. They passed business back and forth to each other, helping to increase visibility and reduced their need for cold calling.

I helped Caroline develop a tracking system so she could keep an eye on the contact list she was building. She purchased a subscription to a Customer Relation Management system that helped in building her database. After speaking to other CPA's that networked well, Caroline determined when and how to stay in touch with her new contacts. She stuck to her system and continued a steady program of follow-up.

Then the magic started to happen. One new client, led to two new clients, which led to five new clients. Caroline was a superstar networker. In her Exclusive Networking group, she was passing and receiving the most referrals every week. She was experiencing the law of reciprocity. People wanted to give Caroline a referral.

By December of that year, Caroline had thirty new clients. When tax season began, Caroline and her partner had to bring on additional help just to make it through the season.

I didn't see Caroline for a few months. We had coffee together one morning in the summer. She talked about being involved in an organization that supports woman entrepreneurs and was becoming very active. She told me she didn't know how she had ever worked without networking before. Caroline was extremely pleased with the level of business she was building, and then she exclaimed that the great relationships she developed through networking was a benefit she never expected.

Notes

_____

_____

_____

_____

_____

_____

_____

_____

_____

_____

_____

_____

_____

_____

_____

_____

_____

Conclusion

This book was written for you, my fellow networkers and future networkers. Building a word of mouth business can seem more difficult than it actually is. I know this first hand. Initially, I thought it was going to be difficult. Then I discovered it isn't.

I promise, when you begin to attend networking meetings on a regular basis, you will meet some of the most wonderful people in your life. But it is important that you open yourself up to new relationships, both business and personal. Some of the greatest people I have ever known came into my life as a result of networking.

I have generated more business than I can fathom as a result of networking and referral partnerships. I found mentors, confidants, referral sources, referral partners, friends, coaches, vendors and most importantly, clients, all as a result of networking. You will too.

In closing, remember three of the most important things in networking.

1. Follow Up
2. Follow Up
3. Follow Up

JOSEPH NOVARA

Special Bonus From Joe

I am so happy you purchased this book. It shows that you are serious about taking your Word of Mouth marketing program to the next level. I want to send you a special bonus that will help you on your way to Word of Mouth marketing greatness.

To receive your special bonus, simply register here:

www.joenovara.com/bookbonus

Shortly after you register, you will receive my "Referral Partner Form". I developed and have used this form for years to keep a list of my best referral sources and partners. This form has been especially handy in following up with promised referrals.

***As an added bonus, I will also include a free download of my "Networking Tips Report".

If you have any questions about developing a Word of Mouth business, email me at **joe@joenovara.com**.

Contact me at the same email address for availability for speaking, workshops and coaching.

JOSEPH NOVARA